Hello!
I am an elephant.

I0108782

Elephants have great memories. They can remember places, other elephants, and even humans they have met.

I know you.

I like to eat grass, leaves, bark, fruits, and roots.

Elephants are herbivores. That means they only eat plants.

I can eat hundreds of pounds of food every day.

Elephants find shading spots to hide from the sun on hot days.

They also flap their ears to cool down.

Elephants also play in water to keep cool in hot weather.

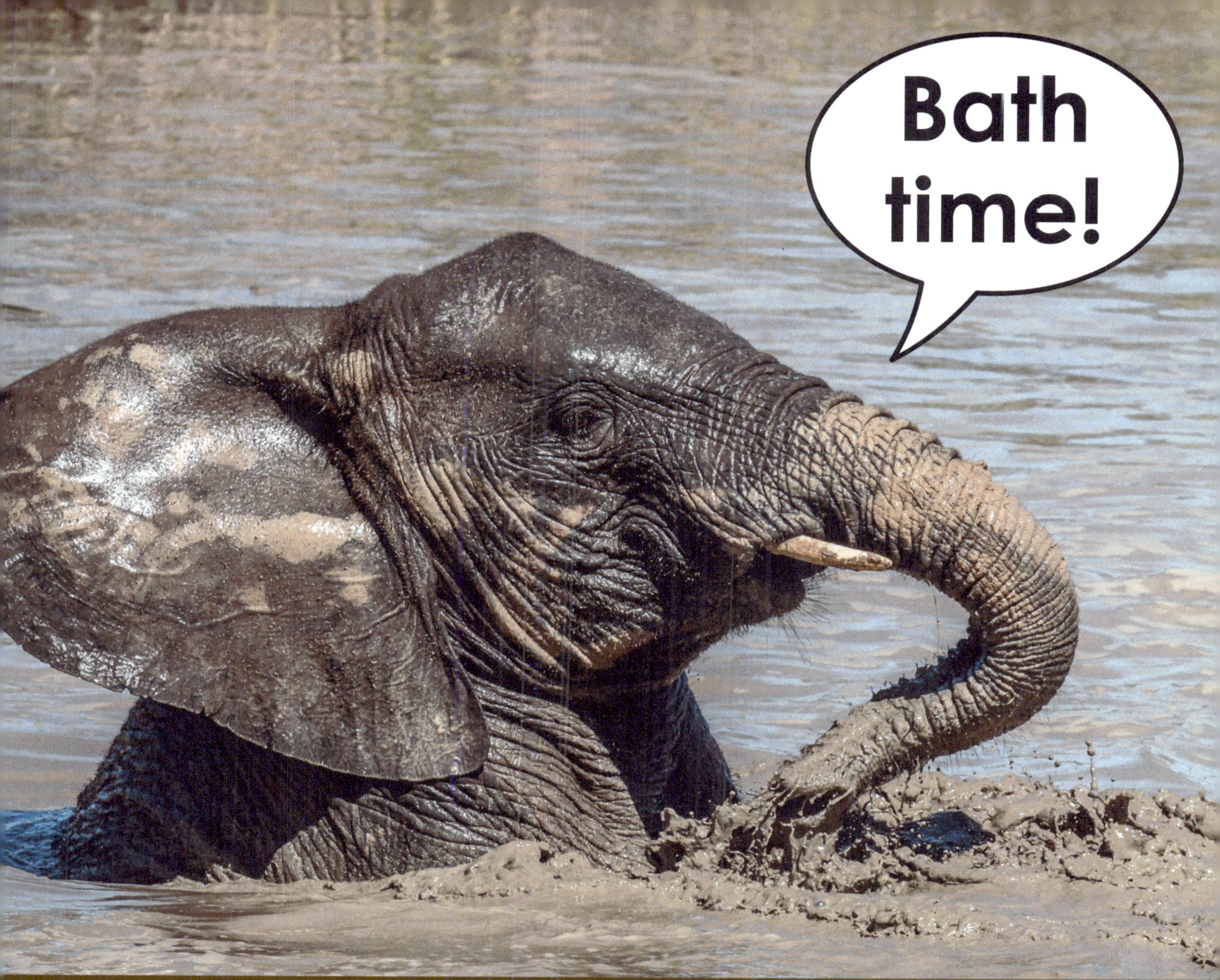

Swimming also helps elephants to keep their skin clean.

Elephants are excellent swimmers.

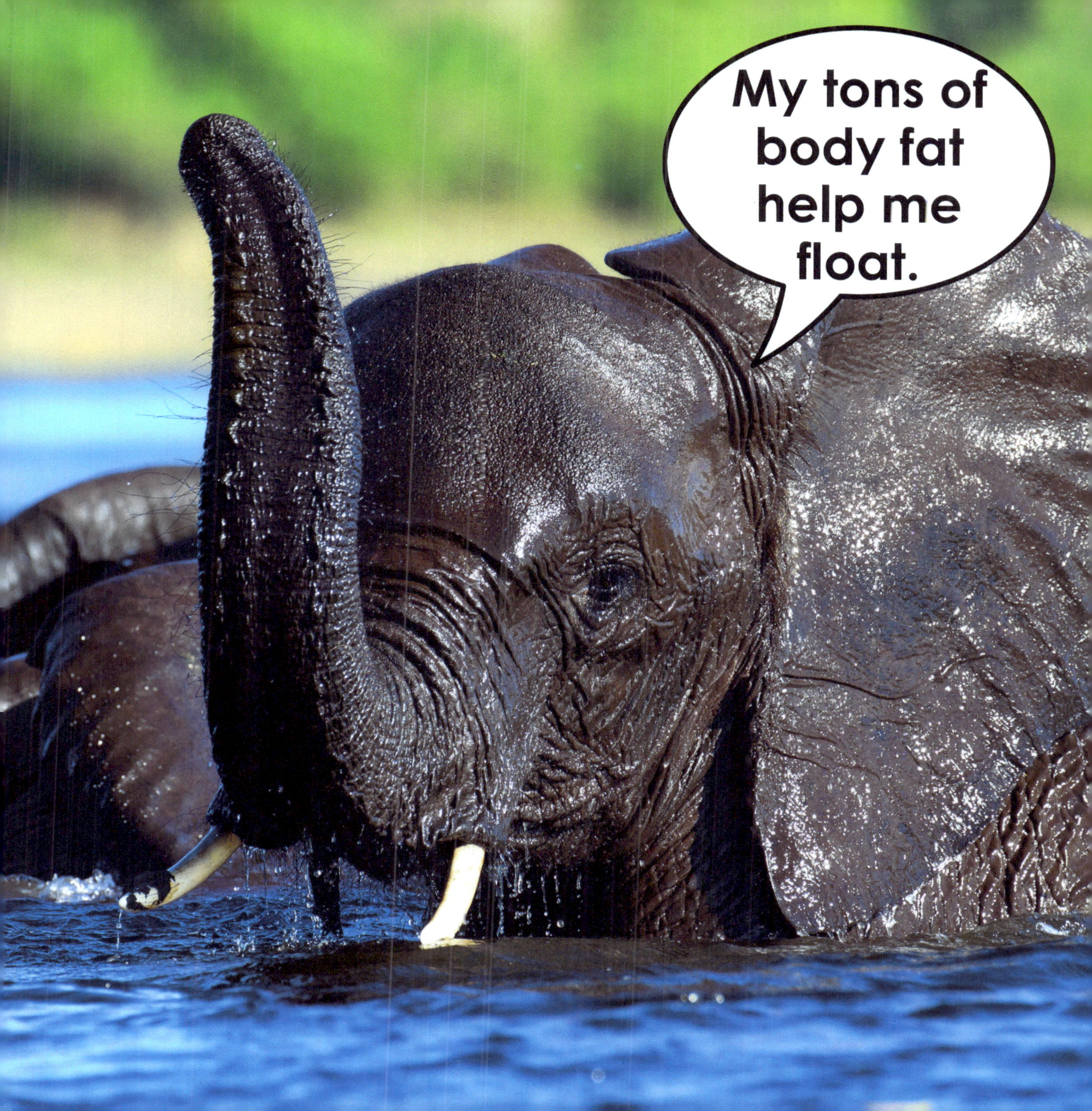
My tons of body fat help me float.

sniff

Elephants have long trunks that they use for breathing, smelling, drinking, and picking up food.

Trunks are also great for snorkeling in the water.

Elephants communicate using various sounds, such as trumpeting, rumbling, and growling.

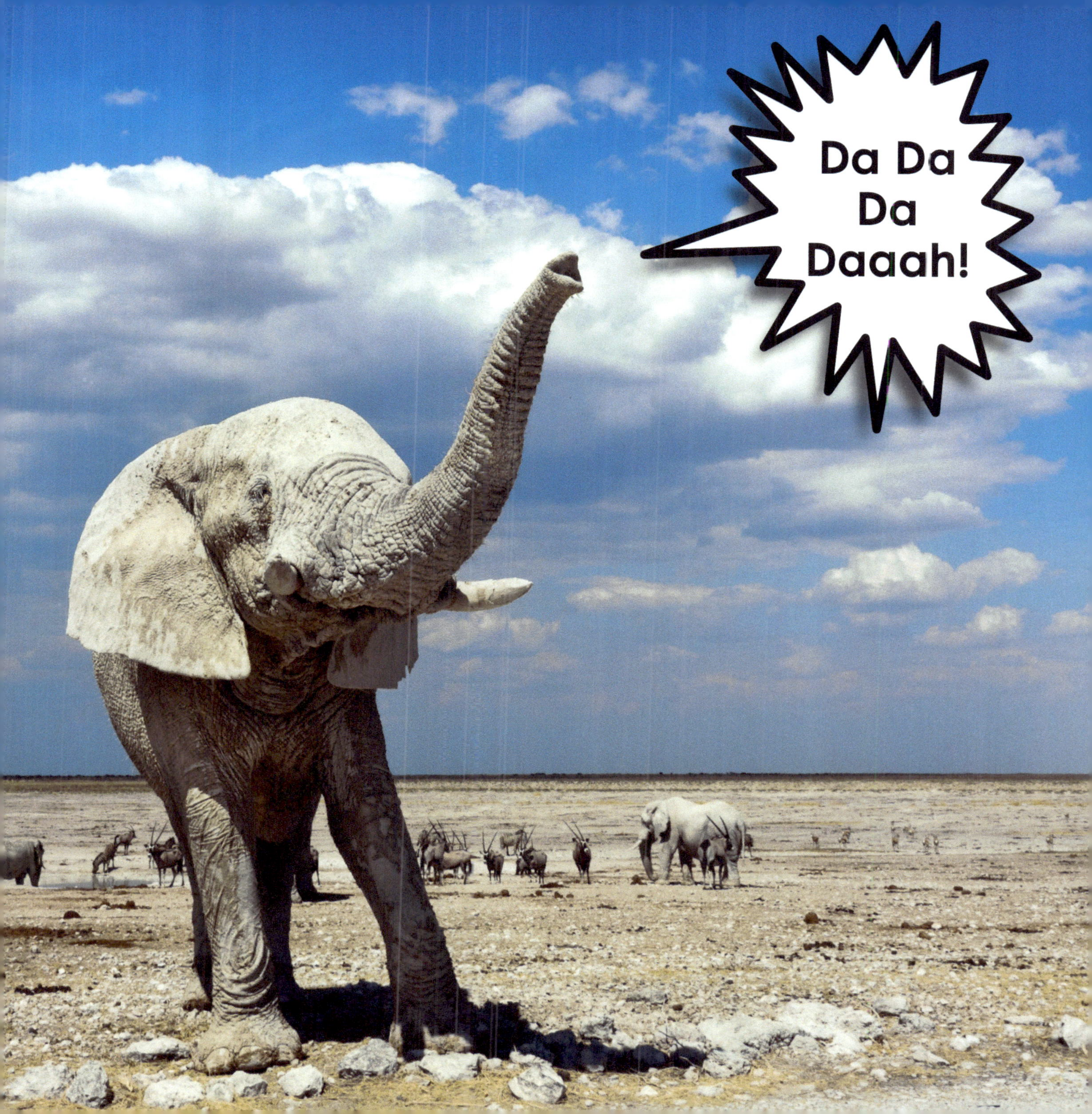
Da Da Da Daaah!

Elephants have very strong legs and can run at speeds of up to 25 miles (40 km) per hour.

The leader of an elephant herd is usually the oldest female.

Where's grandma going?

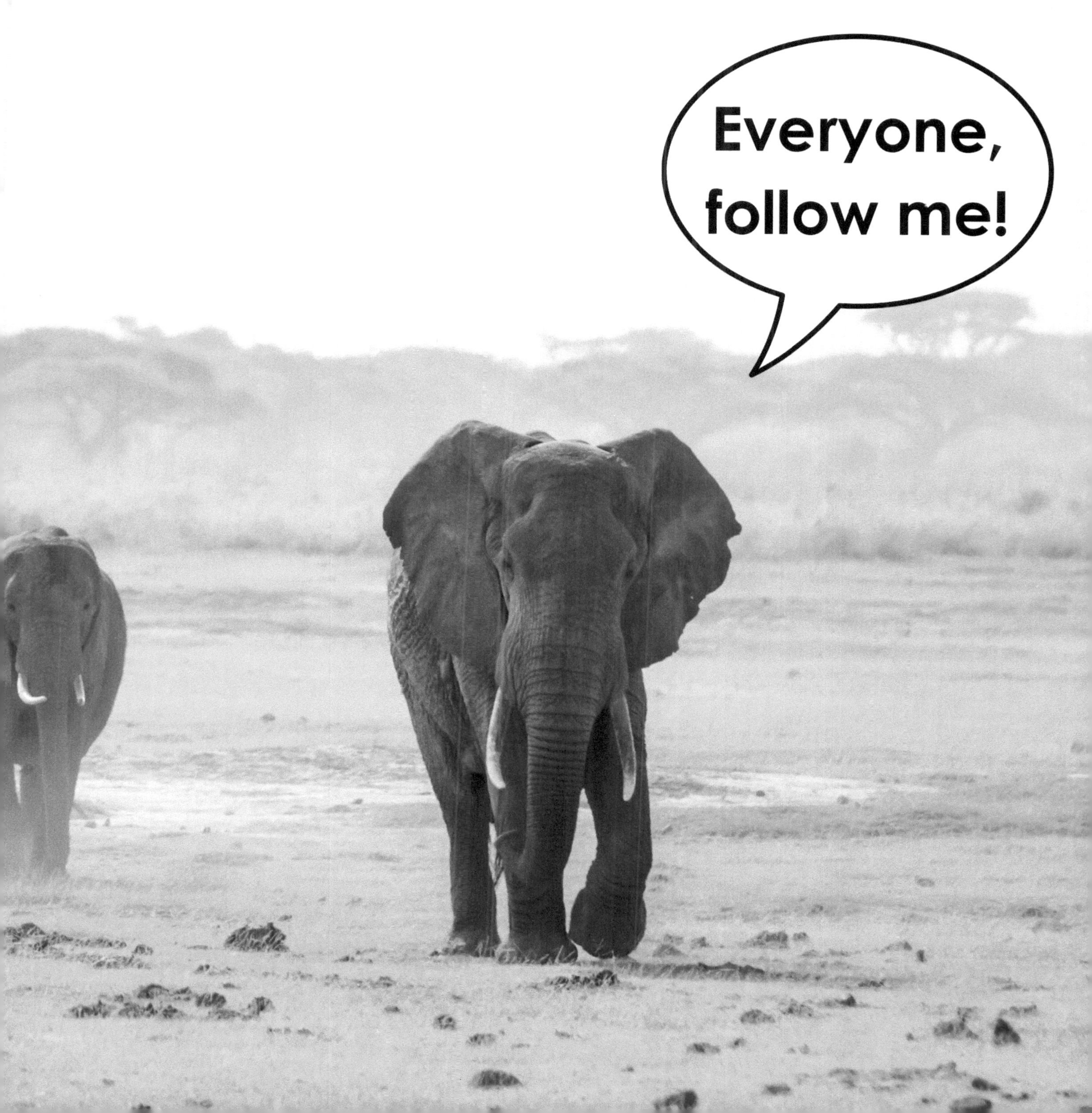
Everyone,
follow me!

Baby elephants are called "calves".

We weigh around 200 pounds (90 kilograms) when we are born.

All the adult elephants help take care of the calves, teach them important skills, and protect them from danger.

I'm here for you.

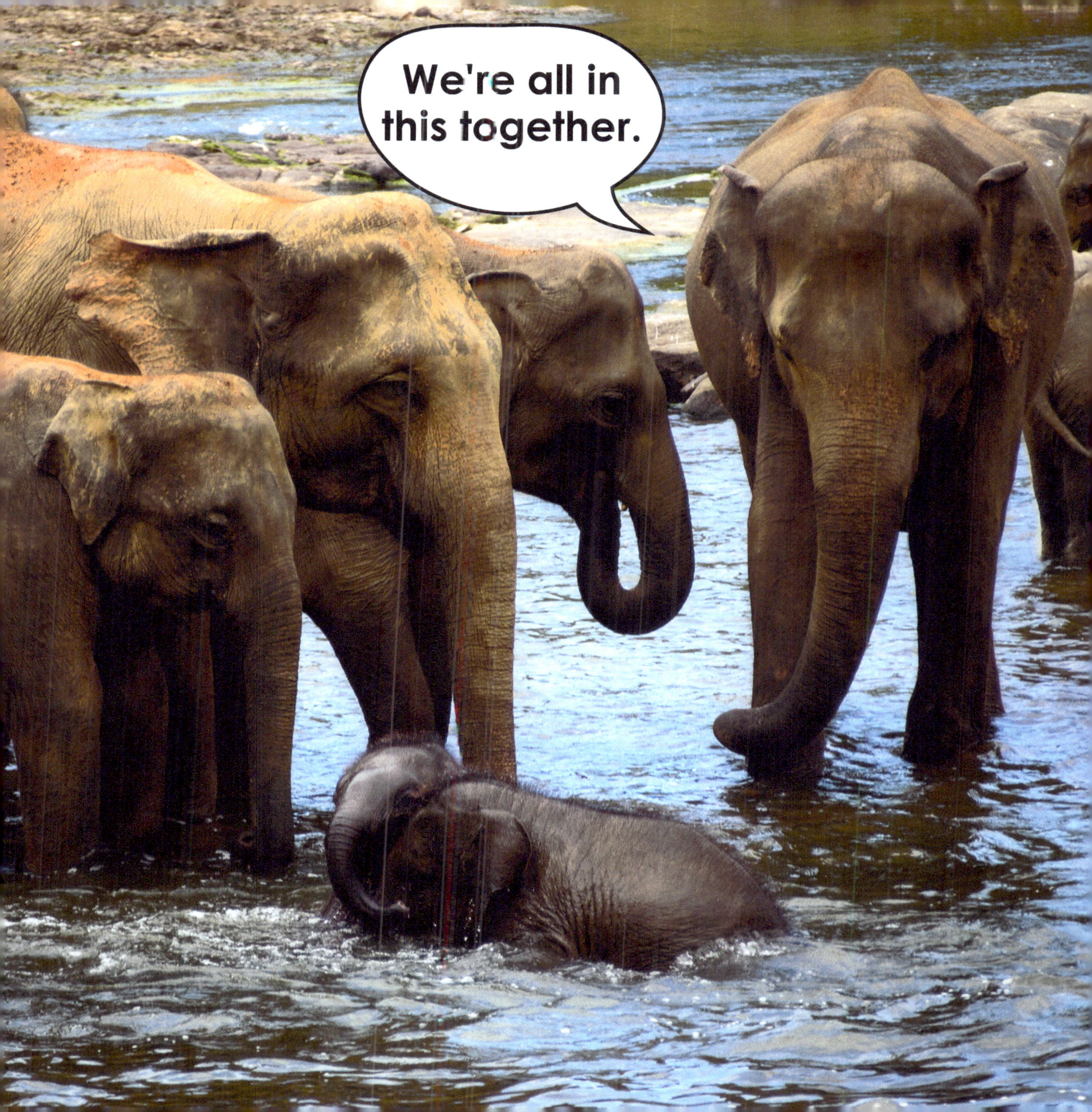
We're all in this together.

Elephants have a unique way of showing love and friendship.
They wrap their trunks together.

It's called "trunk-holding."

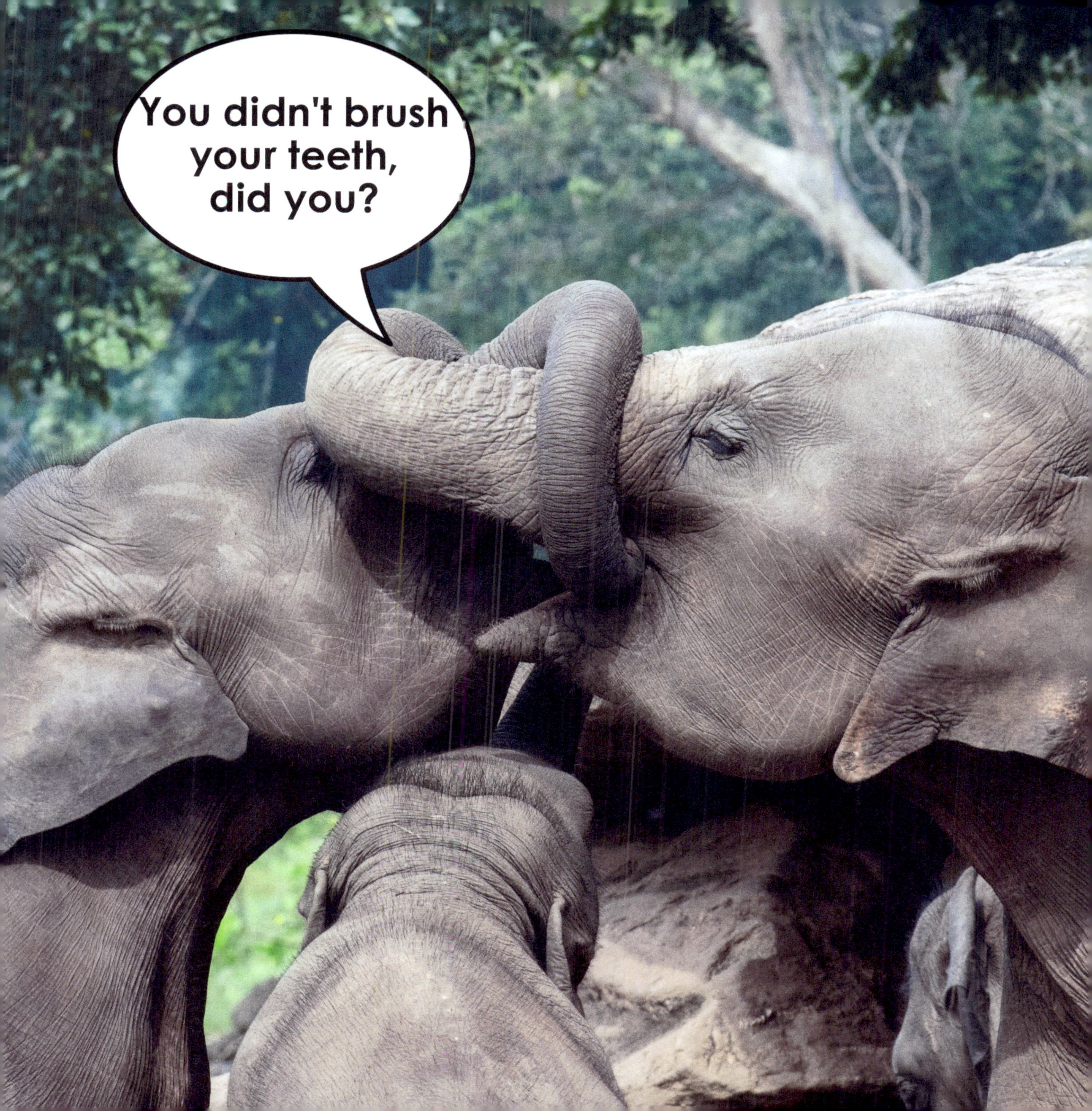
You didn't brush your teeth, did you?

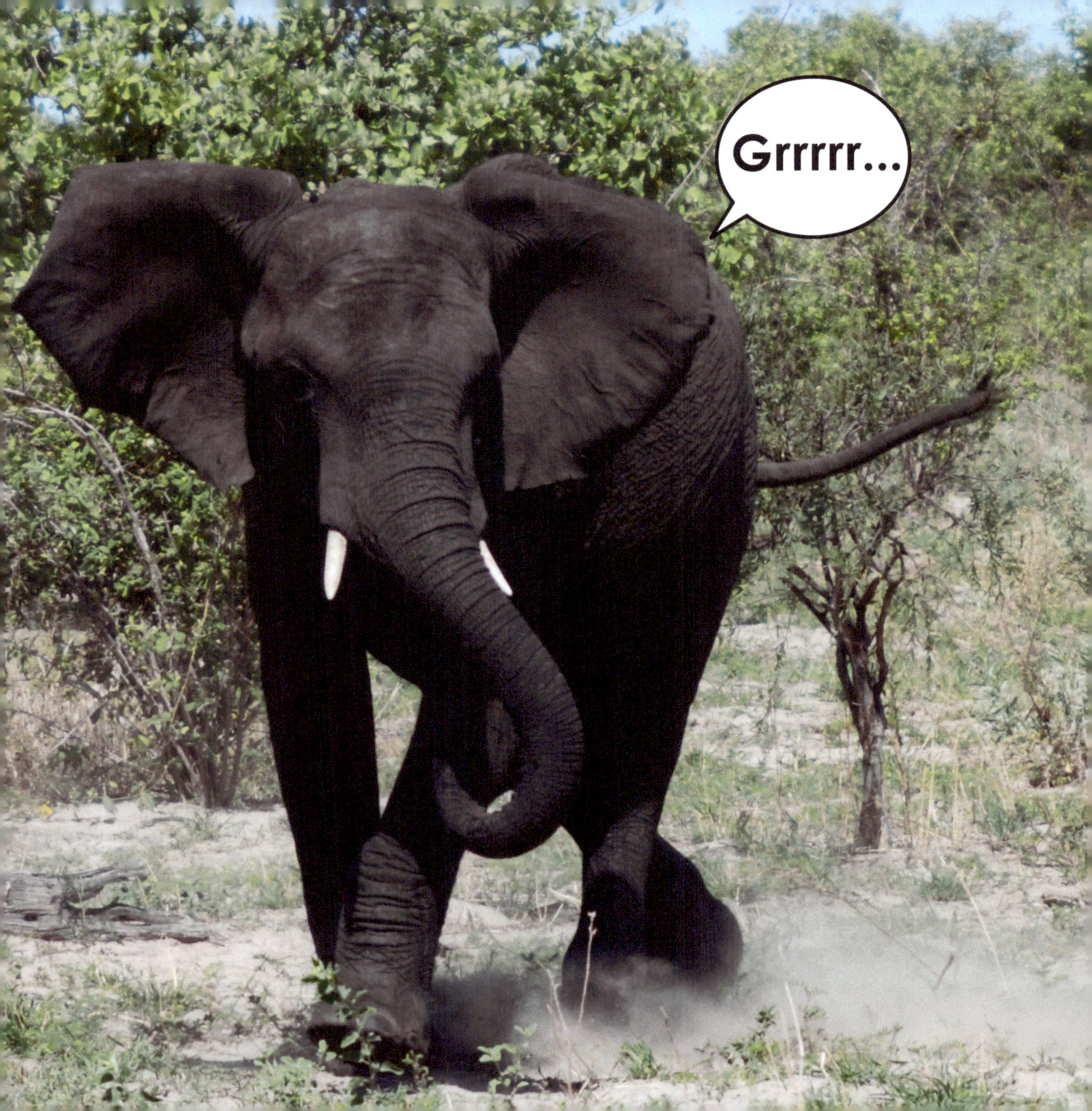
Grrrrr...

Elephants are gentle animals, but they can become aggressive if their herd is in danger.

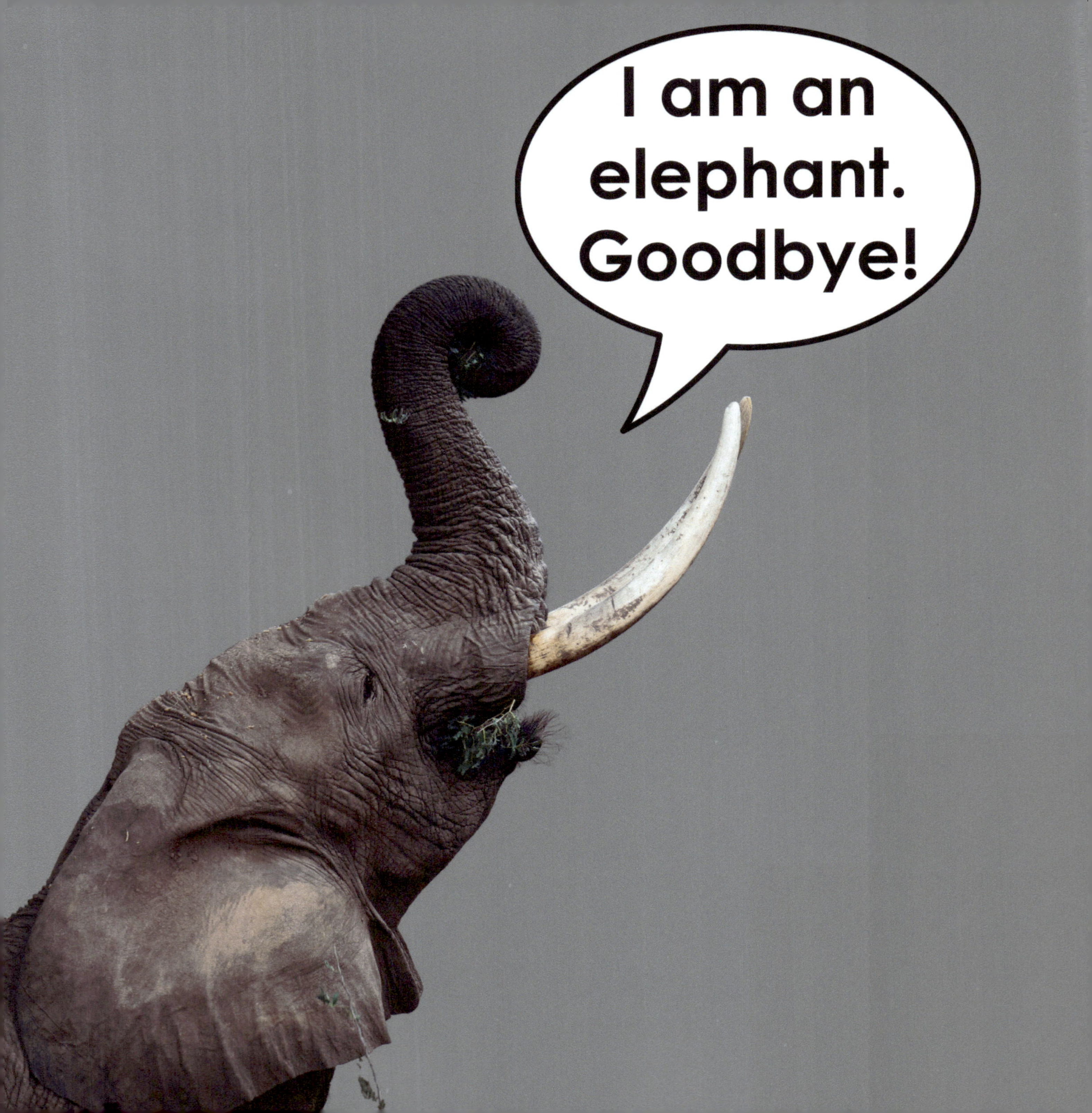
I am an elephant. Goodbye!

Want more?

... and more

Hello parents!

Visit us to find out about new releases and *FREE* offers. We'll let you know when we have a new release coming out and how you can get it for FREE.

And you can cast your vote for what book we make next!

scan here

or visit here

ActiveBrainsBooks.com

---

scan here

Let us know what you think. As an independent publisher, your honest reviews mean a lot to us and our business. We'd love to hear from you!

amazon.com/review/create-review/

or visit here

FOLLOW US on Amazon.

amazon.com/author/activebrainsbooks

ActiveBrainsBooks.com

ACTIVE BRAINS

www.ingramcontent.com/pod-product-compliance
Lightning Source LLC
Chambersburg PA
CBHW042057040426
42447CB00003B/260

9 781957 337470